Original title:
Verdant Voices

Copyright © 2025 Creative Arts Management OÜ
All rights reserved.

Author: Ophelia Ravenscroft
ISBN HARDBACK: 978-1-80567-254-8
ISBN PAPERBACK: 978-1-80567-553-2

Chants of the Ancient Oak

In the shade of an old oak,
Squirrels throw nuts like a joke.
They chatter and giggle in glee,
While branches sway, wild and free.

A wise owl with glasses so thick,
Reads stories that make others tick.
Every night, he hoots with delight,
Sharing tales till the morning light.

Rhythms of the Flourishing Foliage

The leaves dance a jig in the breeze,
Tickling the branches with teasing ease.
A beetle taps out a funny beat,
While ants form a row for a parade treat.

Daisies gossip, in soft, secret tones,
About the antics of bouncy garden gnomes.
They plot to prank the cat in the sun,
With a splash of water—oh, what fun!

Harmonies Beneath the Canopy

Beneath the trees where shadows play,
A raccoon sings at the close of the day.
His warble's off-key yet full of cheer,
Making the critters all whistle near.

The grasshoppers join in a chorus so loud,
While mushrooms nod, feeling quite proud.
Each note tickles the leaves overhead,
As laughter rings out where the brave are fed.

Ballad of the Blooming Garden

In a garden where flowers all prance,
Tulips declare it's a grand romance.
A bee stumbles, tips over a rose,
And giggles erupt where nobody knows.

Sunflowers laugh at the clouds overhead,
Joking that storms have lost some thread.
They twist and they turn with a wink so sly,
Planting giggles as butterflies fly.

Soundtrack of the Seasons

The springtime sings with frogs in shoes,
While summer's buzz is bees with cues.
Autumn's leaves do a silly dance,
And winter's chill makes snowmen prance.

Each season swaps its playful tune,
Like nature's laugh beneath the moon.
With every breeze, a giggle flows,
A symphony where laughter grows.

Echoing Roots

Roots of laughter stretch deep and wide,
Tickling the soil where secrets hide.
Echoes of giggles lift from below,
As worms tell jokes about garden woe.

The trees join in, a chuckling choir,
With whispers that spark delight and fire.
A network of fun, beneath the ground,
Where every punchline can be found.

The Quietude of the Underbrush

In the underbrush, a squirrel pranks,
Making the bushes sway with thanks.
A rustle here, a rustle there,
Nature's jesters fill the air.

With sneaky leaps and zany bounds,
They giggle at the lost and found.
Frogs in tuxedos croak out a cheer,
As rabbits join in, holding their beer.

Cadence of the Canopy

Beneath the boughs, the toucans tease,
With playful banter drifting through leaves.
They swing and sway like silly clowns,
As monkeys mimic all the sounds.

The heights are filled with giggly glee,
Branches bounce in a reverie.
A cascade of joy from tree to tree,
A canopy where fun runs free.

Resonance of the Rushing Stream

The brook babbles loud, oh what a sight,
Fish do the tango, thinking it's night.
Frogs croak their tunes, a splash in the stream,
Even the rocks join in, it seems!

A turtle's a DJ, spinning with glee,
While dragonflies dance like they're on TV.
A water snake slithers, ready to groove,
In nature's dance party, everyone's smooth.

Poems of the Pastoral Life

The cows wear sunglasses, oh such a breeze,
Grazing with style, munching on cheese.
Chickens do yoga, balancing well,
In the barn's corner, they echo their spell.

Sheep play charades, on the green grass,
While goats tell jokes, as they all pass.
The farmer just laughs, pouring some tea,
Chasing the ducks in a wild jubilee.

Echoes from the Fern-fringed Path

Ferns whisper secrets, rustling with mirth,
As squirrels tell tales of the great earth.
A mushroom in polka dots stares with a grin,
Declaring to all, let the fun begin!

The path winds and giggles, a twist here, a turn,
With every step taken, old memories churn.
The sun winks down, a light-hearted jest,
Nature's own laughter, a joyous fest.

Dialogue with the Dappled Light

Sunbeams play hide-and-seek among the trees,
It tickles the daisies with the lightest of tease.
The shadows respond with a chuckle and cheer,
Creating a game for the critters that near.

A squirrel in a top hat, so classy and bright,
Chirps witty remarks in the fading daylight.
The fireflies light up like stars in a row,
As the woods come alive with a magical show.

Chants of the Living Earth

The trees gossip louder, don't you know?
Squirrels hold meetings, and raccoons put on a show.
Frogs sing the blues, while crickets bring cheer,
Even the grass gets giggly this time of year.

Clouds loom above, their puffs like balloons,
They trade silly faces, making goofy tunes.
Wind whispers secrets to the leaves' ears,

Nature's a comedian, let's give her some cheers!

Melodies Among the Foliage

The flowers wear hats in a colorful spree,
While ants march to rhythm, like a tiny decree.
Bumblebees buzz with a comical flair,
Trying to dance without losing their hair.

Birds crack up branches, their jokes take flight,
They mimic each other, from morning till night.
The sunbeams crack silly, tickling trees,
Nature's a stand-up with antics like these!

The Harmony of Blossoms

Petals are chatting, swapping old tales,
The daisies gossip like they're on sail.
Butterflies flutter, laughing in line,
Painting the garden, a canvas divine.

Tulips groove low, while daffodils sway,
Humming a tune that won't fade away.
Laughter is blooming, it's infectious and bright,
With blossoms in chorus, oh what a sight!

Nature's Resonant Heart

The mountains shout snippets of jokes from the past,
    Every echo resounds, but nothing's too fast.
    Streams chuckle softly, the pebbles all grin,
    Dancing in water, oh where to begin?

    Pine trees sway joyfully, tips tickle the sky,
    As flowers rise up, "We're having a pie!"
    Nature is jiving, let's not miss the beat,
We'll dance like the leaves, twirling to the heat!

Poetic Echoes from the Briar Patch

In the thicket where brambles grow,
Rabbits laugh at a slippery toe.
The squirrel mocks with a cheeky dance,
While the hedgehog ponders his chance.

A bird above sings a silly tune,
As ants march along, wearing hats of the moon.
The flowers giggle, they tickle the breeze,
And even the rocks roll with gleeful ease.

A snail shouts, 'Catch me, if you can!'
But the quick little bugs have a better plan.
With whispers and chuckles, the night takes its turn,
As fireflies light up with a spark and a burn.

Laughter lingers in the tangled maze,
In the briar patch, it's a world of plays.
Where nature's peculiar becomes the norm,
And everyone's antics make the forest warm.

The Nature's Soundtrack of Stillness.

Beneath the trees in quiet repose,
A grasshopper practices his stand-up prose.
The crickets chirp in a comedic zone,
While a butterfly giggles on her throne.

With murmurings soft from the whispering leaves,
A deer rolls her eyes at a joke that she thieves.
The stream chuckles lightly as it hums along,
While the rocks join in for a boulder-bound song.

In stillness, the humor of nature unfolds,
With tales of the brave and the timid retold.
A porcupine's quills, they shine with delight,
In this grand symphony, laughter takes flight.

A world where the animals all play their parts,
Crafting a melody that triples our hearts.
In the rustle of grass, the laughter will dwell,
In nature's own tape, all stories will tell.

Whispers of the Green Canopy

Under the shelter of lush leafy arcs,
A chipmunk jests with curious sparks.
The owls hoot jokes from high in the limbs,
While the sun sneaks peeks at the playful whims.

Vines twist in laughter, a wobbly trap,
While a beetle takes stage for a confident clap.
The wind teases softly through branches triumph,
As blossoms shine brightly in nature's own hymn.

Amid the green where the giggles abound,
A turtle's slow waddle is the craziest sound.
Each leaf dances joyfully, swaying with glee,
In a canopy choir full of mischief and spree.

Where whispers of green bring bright chuckles near,
And the shadows play tricks that bring forth a cheer.
In the world of the trees, where humor is grand,
Nature's embrace gives a wink and a hand.

Echoes in the Leafy Sanctuary

In the sanctuary of whispers and greens,
A raccoon shares tales of his midnight scenes.
The owls crack up at his sneaky escapades,
As vines twist together for comedic charades.

With dappled light filtering through the tall fronds,
A family of frogs is caught making ponds.
Their jumps are a dance, all clumsy and loud,
While the butterflies giggle, feeling so proud.

The breezes carry quirks of the day,
Where the thistles and thorns have their own strange play.
A hedgehog tells stories with a twist of a quill,
As laughter erupts from the heart of the hill.

Within this leafy dome, the joy is in bloom,
Where every misstep can light up a room.
In echoes of chuckles that never grow old,
The sanctuary thrives in tales to be told.

The Song of Swaying Grass

The grass has grown quite tall and sly,
It tickles ankles as folks walk by.
In whispers soft, it shares a joke,
A dance-off with the breeze, who spoke?

The daisies giggle, in polite delight,
While dandelions tease, oh what a sight!
With roots that wiggle, they make a fuss,
And clap their hands, what a lovely bus!

The wind starts laughing, a merry croon,
As blades of green hold a grand saloon.
A party ensues where no one's shy,
With grasshopper DJs that jump and fly!

So come and join the grassy spree,
Where joy grows wild and spirits are free.
In this tall haven, where fun's a must,
You'll leave with laughter, and grass in your dust!

Serenade of the Emerald Woods

In the woods where squirrels play chess,
Mushrooms gossip in armor, no less!
A turtle's lost but oh what glee,
He's found some acorns for his tea!

The bushes quake with laughter loud,
As crickets chirp a tune so proud.
The trees do sway in harmony,
As if they're part of a comedy!

An owl hoots out, a punchline clear,
With bated breath, we lean in near.
He cracks a joke about the sun,
We laugh so hard, we're almost done!

So wander deep where the merriment grows,
In emerald woods where anything goes.
With every step, a chuckle in sight,
A symphony of joy that lasts the night!

Lullabies of the Growing Earth

Beneath the soil, a party brews,
Worms wear hats, oh look at their shoes!
They're dancing circles, round and round,
To beats from roots deep underground.

The seedlings yawn with sleepy grins,
While spiders weave some twinkly fins.
Crickets serenade with gentle care,
A lullaby for plants unaware!

The sun peeks in with a cheeky wink,
As raindrops tap a playful link.
A chorus hums, the earth's delight,
Creating rhythms throughout the night!

Join in the dream of nature's play,
As every leaf has something to say.
In this cozy nook where giggles stir,
Lullabies of mirth shall always occur!

Melodies in the Meadow

In the meadow where the butterflies tease,
Flowers bop gently in a soft breeze.
A bumblebee buzzes a jolly song,
While daisies sway and twirl along!

The grasshoppers join in, with legs so spry,
Each leap they take gets a cheer from the sky.
The sun joins in, giving a grin,
As shadows dance, let the fun begin!

A picnic spreads with ants in a rush,
Stealing crumbs, oh what a fuss!
The meadows laugh, a vibrant prank,
As flower crowns fill with dirt, oh dang!

So frolic among the giggling blooms,
Where every flower bursts into tunes.
In this bright place where joy does reign,
The melodies echo again and again!

The Lexicon of Lushness

In a garden where gnomes hold court,
The daisies dance like they're at sport.
While worms debate in fancy dress,
The roots are rich; it's quite a mess.

The ferns gossip in leafy tones,
While ladybugs hide on their thrones.
A snail's slow jog, a gear unwound,
In this green world, all laughter's found.

Trills in the Thicket

A bird sings loud with a crooked beak,
Its notes are bright, though the pitch is weak.
The squirrels cheer, they clap their paws,
"A concert!" they yell, "Let's give them applause!"

The bushes whisper, secrets shared,
With giggles like rustling leaves, they dared.
A raccoon jokes, "Let's start a band!"
In this thicket, fun is always planned.

The Glistening Glade's Tale

In the glade where glimmers wink,
The flowers plot and frogs all stink.
A butterfly, wearing a top hat,
Swayed to rhythms, oh what of that!

The squirrels spun tales of nutty delight,
While fireflies danced, soft sparks in flight.
"Join us!" they laughed, "It's a glowing spree!"
In this tale, fun is the key!

Phrases of the Petal Parade

On a float made of blooms, the petals prance,
With bees as the band, they lead the dance.
A daffodil challenges a dandelion,
"Bet you can't twirl in perfect alignment!"

The sunflowers grin, their heads held high,
While grasshoppers leap, oh my, oh my!
In this parade, all critters unite,
With laughter and joy taking flight.

Harmonies of the Verdant Realm

In the garden, frogs croak a tune,
While bumblebees dance like a cartoon.
The daisies bow to the wind's jest,
As squirrels play tag, not one taking rest.

Rabbits hop, sporting hats too bright,
And ants hold parades, what a silly sight!
The trees join in with a rustling cheer,
Waving their branches, "Come join us here!"

Odes to the Silent Woods

In the woods where shadows play peek-a-boo,
A woodpecker's drum makes the squirrels go 'Ooh!'
Mushrooms wear caps, all fancy and round,
While raccoons trade secrets, never a sound.

The owls tell jokes that only they know,
While the bushes shake with giggles and woe.
The wind whispers softly, it's tickling trees,
As laughter erupts, carried off by the breeze.

Nature's Intimate Confessions

A snail with a plan, moving quite slow,
Tells a tale of a race that set the world aglow.
A worm with a grin sneaks into a dance,
While the lilacs perfume the whole place with romance.

Ladybugs chat in their polka-dot coats,
Plotting their antics, as cheeky as goats.
Trees gossip their leaves, oh such a delight,
Sharing the stories of day and of night.

The Symphony of Sowing Seeds

The seeds in the soil have a grand little chat,
"I bet I can sprout faster - oh look at that!"
The carrots roll over, playing hide and seek,
While peas on a trellis sing tunes that are chic.

A sunflower smiles, standing so tall,
Critiquing the clouds, "You really can't sprawl!"
As rain drops in rhythm, they dance in the breeze,
Nature's own concert, with laughter and ease.

Speak

In the forest where trees conspire,
The squirrels gossip, oh so dire.
A rabbit hops with a silly grin,
While raccoons dance like they're in a spin.

The owls hoot jokes from high above,
While frogs sing ballads of lost love.
Each breeze carries giggles from the leaves,
And laughter rustles through the eaves.

Green Earth

The grass is ticklish, don't you see?
It laughs when you step, 'Oh, let me be!'
Flowers flip their petals, waving hi,
While daisies plot to reach the sky.

A worm recites poetry from below,
His rhymes bring smiles to the garden row.
Even the rocks have stories to tell,
Of garden parties, where all is well.

Verses from the Nature's Heart

The brook babbles secrets with a splash,
While fish giggle, making a dash.
In the thicket, a bear tries to dance,
And the bees buzz in a merry prance.

The sun sneaks in with a playful tease,
Tickling shadows beneath the trees.
Nature's choir sings a silly tune,
Underneath the laughter of the moon.

The Patience of the Ponderosa

The ponderosa stands tall and grand,
But it whispers jokes, oh isn't it bland?
Its bark has wrinkles, like a wise old sage,
Telling tales of a bygone age.

A squirrel clings, laughter in the air,
While he plans a nutty affair.
The ponderosa chuckles, sways in delight,
As branches play tag with the butterflies' flight.

Choreography of the Wildflowers

Wildflowers gather for a dance so bright,
Swinging and swaying in the soft moonlight.
The daisies twirl with a lively shout,
While tulips and pansies prance about.

A bumblebee buzzes, the DJ to all,
Spinning sweet tunes as petals enthrall.
Together they dance, in comical ease,
Painting the world with colors that please.

Anthems Among the Arbors

In trees that sway and twist, so spry,
The squirrels sing, oh me, oh my!
With acorns falling like confetti,
They host a dance, all light and petty.

A raccoon with a top hat prances,
While birds in tune perform their chances,
Each branch a stage, each leaf a note,
They rock the woods, give laughter's coat.

The chipmunks cheer, they shout hooray!
As sunlight spills, the squirrels sway,
With every jump and every twirl,
Nature's jesters in a whirl.

So raise a cheer for wild delight,
In every tree, the world is bright!
These anthems swell from root to sky,
Where humor blooms, oh do not sigh!

The Hush of Hedges

Amid the shrubs, a gossip grows,
With whispers soft, it surely knows,
A hedgehog snores, while others peek,
They must shush him, lest he speaks!

The ivy giggles, twirls with glee,
As rabbits plot a grand esprit,
Their tiny ears much perked to hear,
The secrets flow, like bubbles near.

A rogue raccoon dons a disguise,
In hedges thick, he spies, he lies,
As laughter ripples through the leaves,
With tales of mischief, they believe!

So next time you stroll by the brush,
Just listen in, there's bound to be a rush,
Of giggles hidden in green attire,
In tranquil shrubs, where gossips conspire!

Reflections in the Rain-soaked Soil

Puddles laugh with ripples round,
As worms dance under, revel bound,
With rain boots on, the frogs parade,
In slickest marches, joy displayed.

Wet petals glisten, dew drops wink,
While puddles mirror skies that blink,
A dancing bug, with style so slick,
Goes sliding down, oh what a trick!

The roots below are tickled pink,
In muddy fun, they squish and slink,
An earthworm band strikes up a tune,
With giggly tones that drift to noon.

So join the fun, don't shy away,
In rain-soaked dirt, let laughter play,
With nature's giggles, earthy and bold,
In squishy moments, joy unfolds!

Dialogues in the Dew

In morning light, the droplets chat,
A ladybug in formal hat,
Responds to flowers, bright and loud,
As morning yawns, all nature proud.

The bees buzz secrets, rich and sweet,
While daisies gossip, quite a feat,
With every drop, a story flows,
Of drunken ants and garden woes.

A snail, bemused, joins in the fray,
With slinky moves, he steals the play,
While dew drops giggle on the grass,
Each morning brings a lively class.

So heed the whispers in the air,
For in the dew, delight declares,
With every chat and every turn,
Nature's laughter, we shall learn!

The Tones of Tranquility

In the garden, bugs do dance,
With a bounce and silly prance.
Flowers giggle, leaves do sway,
Nature's laughter brightens day.

Underneath a shady tree,
Squirrels chatter, wild and free.
Birds with jazz, they tweet and sing,
Who knew plants could do such things?

A raucous frog hops on a log,
Mocking the snoozing lazy dog.
Every leaf a giggling sprite,
Tickling breezes, pure delight.

Sunlight flickers, shadows play,
In this merry, green ballet.
Join the fun, take off your shoes,
Nature's joy is hard to lose!

Rhapsody of the Rainforest

In the jungle, frogs compete,
For the loudest, hopping beat.
Parrots squawk, their colors bright,
Dancing through the day and night.

Snakes are twirling, feeling sly,
Sharing secrets with a sigh.
Vines that twist in goofy ways,
Swaying, laughing through the days.

Monkeys swinging from a tree,
Chasing dreams with lots of glee.
Even sloths who move so slow,
Crack a smile, just take it slow.

Rainfall tickles, drops do play,
On the leaves in a fun display.
Join the chorus, it's a scene,
Where wild creatures laugh and preen!

The Serengeti's Secret Songs

Lions lounge, they crack a joke,
While hiding from a silly smoke.
Tall giraffes stretch for dessert,
Nibbling leaves, they look absurd.

Herds of zebras mark their lines,
In a dance of stripes and signs.
Hippos splash and belly flop,
Creating waves, oh what a plop!

Wildebeests with heavy feet,
Join the rhythm, oh so sweet.
In the sun, a lover's quarrel,
Two tortoises in a snail's hurdle.

Underneath a glowing sky,
Nature giggles, oh my, oh my!
Join the wild in laughter's throng,
In this place, where all belong!

Threads of the Thistle

A thistle proud, pricks with delight,
Waves her arms in the morning light.
With a laugh, she tells a tale,
Of bumbles bees who often fail.

Dancing dandelions grin wide,
Sharing secrets, side by side.
Butterflies wearing silly hats,
Flutter by, giving high-fives to cats.

The humble clover, shy yet spry,
Winks at the clouds passing by.
In this haven, chaos reigns,
As nature's humor entertains.

Through the fields, a green parade,
Silly moments never fade.
Join the fun in sunlit glee,
Where laughter blooms, wild and free!

Whispers of the Green Canopy

In the tree's embrace, birds debate,
Squirrels hold court, feeling quite great.
Leaves giggle softly, dancing with glee,
Nature's own jesters are wild and free.

Rabbits in top hats, they prance and pose,
Singing sweet jigs as the party grows.
Frogs leap and croak with delight so loud,
Even the flowers join in, quite proud.

A bug in a tux, loaded with charm,
Shares tales of the woods, causing no harm.
While shadows tease the sun to a game,
The underbrush whispers a secret name.

So come hear the laughter, come join the fun,
In this leafy theater, joy has begun.
With nature's symphony playing all day,
Life's a grand circus, come join the play!

Echoes from the Emerald Depths

Underneath the ferns, a family of mice,
Holds poetry slams, oh, isn't that nice?
With acorns as pens and berries for flair,
Their verses are silly, floating on air.

A turtle on stage plays the slowest beat,
As snails groove along with a melodic treat.
Gophers wear shades, their style on display,
In the emerald depths, hipsters at play.

The pond reflects giggles, so rich and bright,
Fish splash confetti, it's quite a sight!
Amphibians croon love songs to stars,
While crickets provide the cool, jazzy bars.

Laughter hangs heavy, like dew on the grass,
Joy ripples softly, inviting the mass.
In this underwater groove, quirks will abound,
Echoes of glee in nature resound!

Songs of the Mossy Grove

Mossy choir sings in an ancient key,
Toadstools tap dance with utter glee.
The shadows sway to their rhythm so fine,
As whispers of humor in harmony twine.

Inside the grove, a wise old owl,
Tells tales of mishaps with a cheeky scowl.
Each chuckle grows louder, from high to low,
As friends gather 'round for the mossy show.

Hares bounce and spring, their footwork a feat,
While a lazy bear plays a sweet backbeat.
The laughter erupts like a bubbling brook,
Flora and fauna, all lost in the hook.

So gather, you lovers of silly delight,
In the songs of the grove where spirits take flight.
With each note and giggle, friendships will bloom,
Nestled in moss, there's always more room!

Lullabies in Leafy Hues

Breezes whisper secrets to leaves all around,
While critters dance lightly on soft, pillowy ground.
Acorns giggle as they hit the soft chest,
Join in the lullabies, let humor rest.

A chubby chipmunk strums a leafy guitar,
Squirrels twirl in rhythm, who knew they could spar?
Windows of sunlight peek through the trees,
Tickling the branches, a breezy tease.

Up high, the birds perform a high-wire act,
With feathery flaps, they don't look too cracked.
Each note that they sing, a burst of pure fun,
Laughter cascades like rays from the sun.

So come to the glen where the lullabies flow,
In leafy hues where the good vibes do glow.
For every giggle, there's room to spare,
In this leafy wonderland, joy fills the air!

The Language of Leaves

When the leaves start to chatter,
Squirrels raise an eyebrow.
"Did you hear what Pine said?"
"No, but I saw him bow!"

Birch blushed with a rustle,
Ash gave a hearty cheer.
"What's the latest gossip?"
"Maple's lost her deer!"

Whispering branches giggle,
As branches sway in glee.
"It's not just trees that gossip,
The bushes join the spree!"

Nature's little chatter,
Creating laughs galore.
So listen to the forest,
You'll hear jokes and more!

Soliloquy of the Sunlit Grove

In the grove where sunlight dances,
Grass tickles little toes.
"Watch out for that thorny trouble!"
"Too late, I've got a rose!"

The daisies sway and chuckle,
While daisies join the fun.
"Why did the worm cross the path?
To stare at all the sun!"

The shadows play a game,
Of peek-a-boo delight.
"Catch me if you can, dear tree!"
"I'll root for you tonight!"

Laughter fills the branches,
As sunlight starts to blend.
In this grove of cheeky joy,
Comedies never end!

Murmurs of the Verdant Realm

In the realm where green things giggle,
Frogs croak a silly song.
"Did you hear about the lily?
She thinks she's tough and strong!"

The petals share a secret,
"Bees can't dance, you know!"
But all the buzzing buddies,
Are dreaming of a show!

The grass plots a prank,
On a sneaky little hare.
"Hop on over here, my friend,
And prance without a care!"

With giggles in their roots,
The ferns sway from the fun.
Nature's laughter echoes,
Until the day is done!

Symphony of Scented Petals

In a garden full of colors,
Roses put on a play.
"Why did the daisy blush?"
"Because it's flower day!"

The violets chime together,
With tunes of sweet delight.
"Let's dance around the petals,
And twirl till day meets night!"

Amidst the fragrant whispers,
Lilies strike up a jest.
"Do you think the sun will join us?
Or did he lose the quest?"

With petals full of laughter,
They sway in fragrant cheer.
A symphony of blossoms,
That everyone should hear!

The Dance of the Daisies

In a field where daisies jiggle,
They gossip and play, oh what a wiggle!
With petals flapping like silly hats,
They laugh at the bees, and dance with the bats.

Sunshine tickles their bright little heads,
As they spin and twirl, forgetting their beds.
A grasshopper joins with a jubilant leap,
While daisies share secrets, a giggle so deep.

The breeze joins the fun with a swaying flair,
Daisies gossip about the folks in the air.
They've seen quite the drama with clouds overhead,
As they dance like it's the best party yet had.

And when the moonlight comes out for a peek,
Daisies chuckle, feeling quite unique.
Under the stars, they'll sway and they'll prance,
In this floral fiesta, they'll laugh and they'll dance!

The Understory's Soliloquy

In the shadows, a squirrel wears a beret,
With acorns he raps, what a curious play!
He sings to the ferns, who roll with good cheer,
While the mushrooms all giggle, 'He's quite the musketeer.'

'Oh leafy companions, I'm clever and spry,
I'd challenge a raccoon, but he's too sly.
With puns as my weapons, I'll conquer this night,
In the understory, everything feels just right.'

The toadstools applaud, with a clap and a fizz,
As our squirrel performs, he's the star of the whiz.
While crickets harmonize in a whimsical tune,
Even the fireflies twinkle, joining in soon.

So here in the dark, in shadows profound,
The dancers of nature gather around.
With laughter and chatter, they share all their dreams,
In this leafy delight, all is not as it seems.

Hymn of the Heartland

In fields of gold where the cornstalks sway,
The farmers hum tunes while they toil away.
With tractors that rumble and roosters that crow,
They dance to the rhythm of the earth's gentle flow.

A cow with a moo of impressive finesse,
Decides to join in, making quite the mess.
With a laugh from the barn cat, all join in the fun,
As they sing of sweet harvests beneath the warm sun.

The scarecrow starts wobbling, what a sight to see,
With a floppy straw hat, he joins the jamboree.
The chickens are clucking, they've got moves to flaunt,
In a grand barnyard bash, it's their very own jaunt.

As the sun sets low, painting skies bright and grand,
They cherish the moments, a united band.
In the heart of the land, with a giggle and cheer,
They'll raise a glass of cider and shimmy near.

The Sentiments of Seedlings

In a pot so small, a seedling sighs,
With dreams of the sky, under curious eyes.
'Do I really grow tall? Can I reach for the sun?
Or will I just sprout; might as well be fun!'

They whisper and giggle with roots intertwine,
Sharing their hopes over coiled tendrils of vine.
'When I'm finally big, I'll sway in the breeze,
And maybe make friends with the bumblebees.'

A tiny herb hums, 'I'll spice up this soil,
Together we'll flourish, and coax each other's toil.
Let's throw a party for the worms down below,
To celebrate growth; we'll put on a show!'

As rain drizzles down, they all join in glee,
With droplets like jewels, they dance with the spree.
In pots and in gardens, their laughter resounds,
For each little sprout, a new friend surrounds.

The Ethereal Song of the Sowers

In fields where the carrots wear hats so bright,
The peas have a dance that's a comical sight.
The corn gives a giggle, it sways to the beat,
As rabbits play trombones with rhythm so sweet.

The radishes chuckle, they're dressed in their red,
While onions all argue on who's 'best in bed.'
The dirt is a stage, a fine place to prance,
Where veggies delight in their silly romance.

The turnips tell tales, with flair and with flair,
Of bees that wear tuxedos and garden debonair.
And crows sing a ditty, a humorous cheer,
In the game of the crops, fun's always near!

So let's raise a glass, made of foliage green,
To the sassy old garden and all that's unseen.
With laughter and joy, let our hearts plant their roots,
In this patch of pure humor, where nature disputes.

Cadence in the Meadow's Pulse

Bouncing bunnies beat drums, oh what a show,
While daisies are clapping, 'hip hop' in a row.
The crickets are crooning a jazzy refrain,
As squirrels swing by on their comical trains.

The brook plays the bass, with a splash and a gurgle,
While frogs leap in time, doing their own jiggle.
Butterflies twirl in their fanciful gowns,
As nature's full orchestra laughs and astounds.

The grass gets a tickle from ticklish toes,
While wildflowers giggle as soft breezes blow.
Dandelions whistle a tune all their own,
In this quirky green realm, where giggles have grown.

So dance with the daisies, laugh with the leaves,
The meadow's contagious, it's joyful, it weaves.
With pulse and with rhythm, nature's quite grand,
Unfolding her quirks in this whimsical land.

Kisses of the Wind Among the Trees

The trees tell a secret, a whispering tease,
Of leaves that are chuckling, swaying with ease.
A pine with a grin leans over to say,
'Why's an acorn so lonely? It's fun in the fray!'

The wind plays tag, in a hurry it swoops,
It tickles the branches, while nature just loops.
The birch blushes brightly, its bark all aglow,
As the breeze makes it dance to a rhythm, a flow.

Each rustling leaf has a story to sell,
Of owls that crack jokes in their wisdom so well.
With laughter and giggles, the forest's a jam,
Where each sturdy trunk is a jovial slam.

So gather your thoughts in the trees' playful arms,
Their chuckles are treasures, their whispers, charms.
In this symphony sweet, where the wind likes to play,
Laughter drifts gently through the foliage's sway.

The Lure of the Living Landscape

In meadows alive, where the mushrooms all glow,
The grass moves in rhythm, it puts on a show.
The daisies roll laughter, they're bright and they spin,
While toadstools wear grins as nature's folk dance begins.

The hills hold their breath for the tricks at the crest,
Where strawberries giggle, they're truly the best!
The rivers splash tales, like jokes in their flow,
And rocks sit in silence as the laughter won't slow.

The clouds, oh those jesters, they drift 'cross the sky,
Creating formations, a joke passing by.
While sunbeams play peek-a-boo under our feet,
Life's landscape enchants with a rhythm so sweet.

So step on the path where the wildflowers bloom,
Join the chorus of nature, let joy fill the room.
In this quirky expanse, where the wild things engage,
Lies the pulse of the earth, on this glorious stage.

Murmurs Beneath the Boughs

The squirrels chatter, late for a dance,
While acorns roll, given not a chance.
A chipmunk slips, quite full of cheer,
Whispers float, but who can hear?

Leaves giggle in the gentle breeze,
Swaying softly as they tease.
A wise old owl with glasses round,
Scribes tales of what is lost and found.

Frogs croak songs, a wild duet,
With buzzing bees, they're quite upset.
Mother Nature laughs, a silly sound,
As mischief blooms all around the ground.

So join the fun, come take a peek,
Beneath the boughs, we play hide and seek.
With nature's laughter, don't be shy,
In this green playhouse, we're all awry.

The Serenade of the Swaying Grasses

In a meadow, the grasses prance,
Tickled by the wind, they take a chance.
A mouse with shades struts with flair,
While dandelion seeds float in the air.

A butterfly twirls, in a dizzying whirl,
Winks at the bees with a joyous swirl.
The flowers all giggle, what a fine sight,
In this vibrant ballet, oh what delight!

Crickets chirp, holding a beat,
Their tiny legs dance, tapping their feet.
With every tune, the antics grow,
As sunbeams laugh in a warm, golden glow.

So come, let's sway under the sky,
With the silly grasses, we'll laugh 'til we cry.
For in every whisper, a playful tease,
Nature's jesters bring hearts to ease.

Ballads of the Sunlit Glade

In the glade where daisies spin,
A rabbit jokes, wearing a grin.
The sunbeams dance on petals bright,
Join in the frolic from morning to night.

A lizard croons with a raspy tone,
While ants parade, like a marching drone.
The shadows laugh, all hiding away,
As the brook hums tunes of a bright ballet.

Grasshoppers leap with comedic flair,
Waving to flowers without a care.
Each bloom a cheerleader, roots held tight,
In the sunlit glade, everything's right.

So let your worries drift in the breeze,
Join the ballads, do as you please.
For nature's wit is a glorious show,
With laughter and joy in every row.

Soliloquies in the Thicket

Amidst the thicket, a hare recites,
Tall tales of antics in merry nights.
The bushes whisper, gossip unfolds,
As foxes grin with their cunning holds.

A raccoon rolls in giggles and jest,
Crafting mischief, he loves it best.
With every rustle, a chuckle escapes,
As the moonlight plays, and the world reshapes.

The twinkling stars join in the fun,
Winking at creatures, one by one.
In the midnight orchestra, wise owls hoot,
Setting the stage for silly pursuits.

So listen close to the secrets shared,
In the dark thicket, everyone's dared.
With laughter echoing through the night,
These soliloquies bring pure delight.

Whimsical Whispers of Wildflowers

In fields of blooms so bright and gay,
The daisies dance in a cheeky way.
They giggle and bounce, a floral parade,
While bees buzz jokes in the sun's warm shade.

A rose, with a wink, says, "I'm the best!"
But lilies burst out, "We must protest!"
With petals a-flap, they mock and tease,
As butterflies swoop by with the greatest of ease.

The tulips gossip, their colors ablaze,
"Did you see that bee? He's in quite a craze!"
With each little whiff of the pollen they share,
They bumble along without a single care.

As the sun starts to set, and the light's fading fast,
The jokes of the flowers will surely outlast.
With petals so laughable, nature's playlist,
Tonight, even the moon can't resist a twist.

Cadence of the Canopy

In treetops high, where squirrels parade,
Branches burst songs, like a grand charade.
The wind tickles leaves, a chorus so fine,
While chipmunks debate who gets to climb.

With a rustle and rumble, the branches chi-chat,
"I saw a man; he might be a cat!"
The owls laugh softly, their wisdom a cloak,
Winking at creatures who jump and joke.

A funny old crow caws, "What's that up there?"
"Just a human!" squeaks a critter in despair.
The acorns chuckle, "We'll drop in a while,"
As the forest giggles, each tree wears a smile.

The shadows grow long under twilight's embrace,
The canopy whispers with humor and grace.
Nature's ballet, in laughter we trust,
With each rustling leaf, wander dreams turn to dust.

The Songbird's Serenade

In the morning light, the chorus begins,
With chirps and whistles, a warbling win.
A robin mocks, with a dance in the air,
While finches, in tutu, give quite the flair.

The sparrows debate who's done the best trill,
A blackbird lounges, nonchalant and chill.
With a flick of their tails, they tune up the skies,
As the cat at the window rolls its big eyes.

The nightingale swoops down with a groove,
"I'm the headliner, let's show off our move!"
While mockingbirds copy, in playful intrigue,
Their songs cause a ruckus, a melody league.

As dusk turns to dark, they wrap up the show,
With a final crescendo, in a burst of glow.
Nature's own band, so funny and free,
Reminding us laughter is key in a tree.

Interludes in the Green Embrace

In meadows wide, where the grass tickles toes,
Beneath nature's blanket, a warm breeze flows.
The daisies gossip about bees in suits,
While the clover jokes about wearing green boots.

A hedgehog rolls by, with a spiky-laced grin,
"I'm the pokiest friend, let the laughter begin!"
A snail slides in, at a comically slow pace,
"Wait up, sweet hedgie, let's pick up the race!"

Under skies so vast, the giggles grow loud,
As earthworms wiggle, so proud and unbowed.
A rabbit leaps high, doing flips in the air,
"Catch me if you can—oh, wait, I'm not there!"

As dusk brings the hush, the moon grins wide,
In the green embrace, where all fears subside.
Every fern and flower holds secrets to share,
In laughter's soft embrace, we find joy everywhere.

Whims of the Wild

In the meadow, rabbits dance,
With little hats, they take a chance.
Squirrels giggle up the trees,
Share their acorns with the bees.

A raccoon plays a game of chess,
Witty foxes jest and jest.
The owls hoot with playful flair,
While the turtles snore without a care.

Frogs in tuxedos sing a tune,
Underneath the silver moon.
Grassy hills paint silly grins,
Nature laughs while fun begins.

So come and join this wild parade,
Where every creature's unafraid.
With giggles echoing through the night,
In the woods, it feels just right.

The Conductor of the Canes

In the thicket, a stick stands tall,
Leading critters—a grand hall.
With a flick and a swish, a tune plays,
As the trees sway in a jiggy blaze.

The drums are bunnies thumping away,
While the birds chirp, 'Hip Hip Hooray!'
A hedgehog with a baton leads,
As everyone dances, fulfilling their needs.

A breeze joins in, a merry surprise,
Tickling ferns and butterflies.
The reeds sway as they sing along,
In this woodland concert, nothing goes wrong.

So grab a cane and hit the beat,
With twirls and hops, who'll take a seat?
In nature's choir, we'll all unite,
With laughter and joy, oh what a sight!

The Breath of the Blossoms

Petals whisper, 'Come out and play!'
With butterflies on parade today.
A daisy tells a knock-knock joke,
While tulips giggle and softly poke.

Bees wear bow ties, buzzing in time,
As the sun winks—it's all sublime.
Each flower shines with playful glee,
In this garden of laughter, we're wild and free.

The wind teases, 'Catch me if you dare!'
As blooms sway with curly hair.
A sunflower grins and takes a bow,
"Life's too short, just enjoy it now!"

So waltz with petals, twirl and spin,
The joy of spring is where we've been.
In every color, laughter blooms bright,
Nature's giggle is pure delight.

Chronicles of the Cold Moonlight

Once upon a frosty eve,
Snowflakes danced, cannot believe.
A penguin slipped on icy ground,
And laughed aloud with joyous sound.

The owls debated who won the race,
While snowmen giggled with glee on their face.
A polar bear tried to make a pie,
But everything was too cold to fry.

In shadows cast from breezy clouds,
The critters gather, forming crowds.
With ice skates made from twigs and dreams,
They twirl and twist; it's better than it seems.

So join the fun beneath the night,
Where icy cheer warms every sight.
In the moonlight's glow, joy takes flight,
With tales of laughter, it feels just right.

The Narrative of the Nurtured

In a garden thick with chatter,
The carrots argue, "Who's fatter?"
Tomatoes blush, they roll their eyes,
While lettuce laughs at all the lies.

Radishes boast of underground fame,
But turnips grin, they play the game.
Cucumbers whisper, 'We're the best!'
As bees join in for nature's jest.

The gardener grins, holding a spade,
"Looks like dinner's going to be made!"
But veggies giggle with glee and cheer,
Saying, "Not tonight, we've stories to share!"

With each green leaf, and each wild shout,
The garden's a party, no room for doubt.
So next time you're near a patch so bright,
Listen closely, they'll tickle your night.

Breath of the Bramble

In the bramble where the berries jest,
Raspberries tease, 'We're the best!'
Blackberries giggle, their thorns on show,
While wildflowers dance in the breezy flow.

A squirrel prances, tail in the air,
"Who's the fruitiest? Come show some flair!"
A ladybug joins with a tiny spin,
Cheering for those who dare to begin.

The thickets create a raucous roar,
Foxes laugh, they can't take any more.
"Who's tart? Who's sweet?" they chant in delight,
As fireflies wink, lighting up the night.

So next in the bramble, don't take a pass,
Join the laughter in the grass.
For life is a party, and all of us know,
It's better with friends—and a berry or two!

The Muse of Morning Mist

When dawn tips its cap, the dew drops play,
Misty winks surround the day.
A squirrel meditates on a branch,
The fog just giggles, "Take a chance!"

Pansies whisper secrets from their beds,
While daisies dance, flipping their heads.
"Who'll put on a show?" the sunflowers grin,
As rosy fingers stretch to begin.

Hummingbirds zoom for a quick bit of buzz,
While the morning titter tickles with fuzz.
One butterfly flits and says in a twirl,
"Come on, everyone! Let's give it a whirl!"

Each petal sings in morning's embrace,
Nature's humor, a lighthearted chase.
So rise with a smile, let laughter unfurl,
In the mist of the morn, let joy whirl!

Voices from the Verdant Valley

In the valley where the grass loves to chat,
The daisies gossip, "Look at that!"
Clover crowns take turns in their prance,
While the dandelions start a dance.

A wise old oak says, "Don't be a bore,
Let's swap some stories, who's got more?"
The stream giggles softly, splashing around,
"Once I was lost, but now I'm found!"

The poppies declare, "We're the best of the bunch!"
While the sun gets busy, stirring up lunch.
As the breeze sings sweet with a tickle and tease,
All gather 'round to share with ease.

So when you roam through this lively domain,
Listen closely, not a moment is plain.
For in every leaf, and each little sound,
The voices of joy in the valley abound!

The Story of the Sylvan Shadows

In a forest quite lively, shadows prance,
They dance around trees, quite lacking in stance.
With giggles and chuckles, they play hide and seek,
Whispering secrets while playing hide and peek.

A squirrel joins in, with acorn on ear,
Every nutty punchline brings loud bursts of cheer.
The shadows retell tales of trees dressed in green,
Of mischief and magic, well-kept and unseen.

Amidst all the laughter, a brook flows with glee,
Singing songs of the woods, oh so splish-splashy.
Frogs croak in rhythm, with comedic flair,
While fireflies twinkle, lighting up the air.

In this quirky realm where the shadows conspire,
Life's silliness blooms like a never-ending choir.
So take a step in, let your worries unwind,
In the land of the shadows, fun's what you'll find!

The Voice of Vanishing Vines

Vines twist and twirl, in their leafy attire,
They whisper of things like a flirty green choir.
One claims it's a concert, with roots in the ground,
While others just giggle, voicing not a sound.

A snake joins the banter, with jokes up its sleeve,
Slithering 'round, convincing vines to believe.
When asked for a punchline, it gave an old hiss,
"Why did the vine cross? To get to the bliss!"

As leaves start to giggle, the sun hits just right,
The flowers break into laughter, a colorful sight.
The vines start a trend, in their quest for a rhyme,
Setting the stage for a botanical mime.

Their world filled with puns, it's a riotous spree,
With every new twist, there's more laughter for free.
So if you should wander where the green meet and shine,
Join in with the vines, they'll make giggles align!

The Unison of the Understory

Underneath the tall trunks, where shadows reside,
Creatures are chattering, oh what a wild ride!
A raccoon with glasses, taking notes as he browses,
He's writing a book about woodland houses.

A family of rabbits throws wild parties at night,
With carrots for snacks, oh what a delight!
They hop to the rhythm of crickets' loud tunes,
Amidst tales of the stars falling down like balloons.

A wise old owl nods, with a grin on his face,
As underplants giggle in their leafy embrace.
He hoots out, "What's green and hops? A joke just for me!"
The others all chuckle, "Ha! That's too silly!"

In this hidden domain where the laughter won't cease,
The dance of the undergrowth brings gentle peace.
So come join the fray, let your troubles be free,
In the stomping of roots, you'll find harmony!

Melodic Roots

Roots winding and weaving, beneath all the play,
They gossip and tease in their own special way.
One root tickles another, with ribald delight,
A chorus of giggles in the soft, starry night.

The mushrooms all chuckle, with caps all ajar,
"I hear a good riddle, let's raise our bizarre!"
And as the roots hum in their earthy embrace,
The leaves wave along, with a wobbly grace.

Worms twist in the soil, crafting beats with their moves,
As melodies bubble up, and nature grooves.
"Why do trees gossip?" a root quips with glee,
"To spread all the news from the trunk to the spree!"

In this joy-filled abyss, laughter reigns free,
In a symphony woven for all to agree.
So tap your own roots, and let your heart thrum,
In the playful ballet of nature, we're all just a crumb!

Tapestry of Nature's Chorus

The trees are chatting about the best shade,
While squirrels debate on the latest trade.
A frog's got a joke that he just can't hold,
In the sun-soaked glade, the stories unfold.

The flowers gossip, with petals so bright,
They talk of the bee that just took flight.
A snail tells tales of the trickiest path,
While birds laugh out loud with a bubbly laugh.

Mossy rocks nod, they don't miss a beat,
As lizards perform with their fancy feet.
There's humor in every rustling leaf,
And every little critter brings comic relief.

In this vibrant theater, nature's the stage,
Where critters gather to share and engage.
So here's to the chorus, with giggles galore,
In a woodland wonder that never gets poor.

The Lure of the Lush Landscape

A rabbit with style hops over the brook,
While a chipmunk critiques a new fashion book.
The daisies are leaning, quite judgmental,
Murmurs of envy, oh how sentimental.

The dewdrops giggle, they twinkle and shine,
As ants parade through like they're on a line.
A butterfly swoops in with a cheeky flair,
Dancing on breezes without a care.

A cautious tortoise, slow but so sly,
Gives advice to a hare on how to fly high.
And while all this banter is quite the display,
Nature herself joins in on the play.

In this landscape lush where jokes bloom and thrive,
Every root and flower feels so alive.
So come take a stroll, let laughter unwind,
In the joyous embrace of the green and kind.

Refrain of the Roots

The worms in the soil are poets at heart,
Penning their verses while playing their part.
With rhythm in tunnels and rhymes in the dirt,
They giggle at flowers, their bright little flirt.

The roots hum tunes, they wiggle with grace,
As they whisper secrets of the earth's embrace.
A bug struts by in a leafy attire,
Boasting of conquests, lifting spirits higher.

The stones roll their eyes at the grass's green pride,
While the stream chuckles gently, flowing with stride.
Each ripple a giggle, each splash a delight,
Nature's own concert under the moonlight.

In this jovial realm where humor is sown,
Every crevice and cranny feels perfectly known.
So let's raise a cheer for the roots underground,
Where laughter and lore can endlessly abound.

Odes to the Woodland Spirits

The fairies are dancing on mushrooms so round,
They're giggling and spinning, joy knows no bound.
A sprite tells a tale of a ladder to sky,
While winking at owls who wink back, oh my!

The gnomes gather 'round with their stories so old,
Of treasure they found, or so they've been told.
A leaf whispers softly, quite caught in the chat,
While a hedgehog debates between cheese or a rat.

The shadows are buzzing with spirits in flight,
Each flicker of firefly is pure delight.
They jest 'round the campfire with marshmallow dreams,
While twinkling starlight adds to the gleams.

In this woodland realm, laughter fills the air,
With spirits and creatures just having a flare.
So join in the mirth, let your spirit be free,
In the jolly embrace of the trees and the breeze.

Soundwaves of the Shaded Glade

Squirrels argue in the trees,
Debates about the tastiest leaves.
A crow caws like a trumpet's blare,
While rabbits dance without a care.

The wind joins in with a gentle sigh,
Tickling flowers as it passes by.
A frog croaks out a silly tune,
With a little mouse who taps a spoon.

Breezes giggle through petals wide,
As bees buzz low with a polka slide.
The sun peeks in, a cheeky grin,
And all of nature sings to win.

Laughter echoes off tree bark,
As breezes play hide and seek by the park.
In this glade, joy takes its flight,
Where nature's fun shines ever bright.

The Whirl of the Willows

Willow branches sway and twist,
Dancing to a breeze's tryst.
The squirrels spin like acrobats,
While birds wear hats of furry bats.

Grasshoppers leap with style and flair,
As the willow whispers, 'Come join, beware!'
A raccoon whoops, a playful sight,
And chases shadows into the night.

They play tag beneath the stars,
While fireflies glow like tiny cars.
Each leaf that flutters serves a role,
As laughter bubbles, fills the whole.

In this waltz of life and cheer,
Every rustling whisper draws near.
So spin with whimsy, join in the fun,
In the willow's grasp, we are all one.

The Lament of the Leaf Fall

Leaves rain down with a rustle and swirl,
Complaining loud, 'Oh, what a whirl!'
'We once were green, now crispy and brown,
Why can't we just go back to town?'

A leaf squeaks out, 'It's not our fault!'
While another slips off, taking a vault.
They twirl and twist in a clumsy flight,
Wishing for stays in the summer light.

Grounded leaves share a giggle and moan,
As piles of them make a squishy throne.
A squirrel jumps in, gives a little shout,
'What's the fuss? You're a comfy-out!'

In their drama of falling grace,
They find some joy in the messy place.
So let them tumble, frolic, and play,
For laughter lingers on autumn's way.

Reverberations of the Rugged Terrain

On rugged hills, the echoes ring,
As stony critters start to sing.
A lizard leaps with a little thud,
Making ripples in the muddy crud.

Rocks roll by with a playful chat,
While insects groove, 'Imagine that!'
They tick-tock dance on the canyon's ledge,
Mischief bubbles as they all pledge.

The wind howls loud, a comical croon,
Joining the show with a warbling tune.
Mountains chuckle, canyons chime,
In nature's playground, it's all sublime.

With every stomp on the earthy stage,
Laughter erupts, as if from a page.
Join the ruckus; let spirits soar,
In the rugged dance, you'll laugh and roar.

Solstice Songs of the Forest

In the forest all spry and sprightly,
Trees dance with shadows, oh so lightly!
Squirrels steal acorns, what a delight,
While raccoons giggle deep into night.

The owls hoot jokes, they think they're wise,
While fireflies blink like they're in disguise!
Frogs croak choruses, with great aplomb,
Even the grasshoppers tap to the drum.

Leaves rustle secrets, a ticklish affair,
As chipmunks play tag without a care.
A skunk strolls by, with a scent so strong,
But the laughter of nature sings a sweet song.

So gather 'round friends, let's join their cheer,
For in this green space, there's nothing to fear!
Life's silly moments, in riotous bloom,
Under sunlight's grace, we all find room.

The Whisper of Wisteria

Wisteria's giggle hangs in the air,
With blossoms that sway, as if they care.
Bees buzz about, doing their dance,
While petals twirl down, a floral romance.

A butterfly flirts with a leafy young sprout,
Getting lost in a daydream, can't figure it out.
The gardener mumbles, confused and bemused,
As the vines wrap 'round, making him feel used.

In the warmth of the sun, all creatures unite,
With critters and critters, a pure old delight.
And just when they think the show's all but done,
A wild raccoon crashes, steals snacks—oh what fun!

So raise up your glasses to laughter and cheer,
To wisteria whispers that all creatures hear.
With each little giggle and fluttering leaf,
The garden's a kingdom of smiles and relief.

Notes from the Nature's Symphony

In the meadow, a cacophony rises,
Grasshoppers croon as sunlight surprises.
Crickets in tuxedos, they sing through the night,
While symphonic birds put the stars in the light.

A squirrel on stage, in a nutty ballet,
Dodging the crows, getting lost in his play.
With a flourish of tail, a dramatic display,
The chickens all cluck, in their own disarray.

There's a frog playing trumpet, so bold and so brash,
While deer in the back chew their leaves with a splash.
And all of this music, oh, what a delight!
Nature's grand concert, feels just right tonight.

So tap your feet gently to this earthy beat,
From roots to the skies, it's a rhythm that's sweet.
Raise your voice high, let the laughter abide,
In this jolly symphony, let joy be our guide.

The Caress of the Climbing Vines

Climbing vines twist with a cheeky grin,
They scramble and tangle, prepared for a spin.
With tendrils that tickle each passerby,
They whisper sweet secrets while swinging up high.

A raccoon in trouble, caught up mid-crawl,
His little paws waving like he's on a ball!
While snickers from foxes, they echo around,
As laughter erupts from the joys that abound.

Grapes plump and jolly, they sway side to side,
Hoping to witness this grand vine ride.
And when the sunlight starts fading away,
The vines hold a party, to dance and to sway.

So join in the jests, let the fun never cease,
In the garden of glee, may your heart find its peace.
With laughter and light, in nature divine,
The caress of these climbers is simply benign.

www.ingramcontent.com/pod-product-compliance
Lightning Source LLC
Chambersburg PA
CBHW051641160426
43209CB00004B/744